TH MARY DAVIS • LILIAN WILLIEROB DUNCAN • EVA BELLE EDWARDS • MARCELEN
A MIDDLEBROOK • JEANETTA LUCILE MOOREHEAD • MINNIE BELL QUARLES • TES
RNTON • ROSE MARIE ANDERSON • VIRGIE LEE CAYWOOD • ELLA MAE DAVIS • VER
TATUM • RUBY LEE WARD • ESTELLE BERNICE WILLIAMS • BESSIE M. WILLIS • ANNA
LLY ANNA FRAZIER • MATTIE LOU GRAY • JESSIE BOWIE HALL • THELMA PEARLIE JOHNSON • BETTE ELIZABETH MCDONALD • MATTIE
PAULINE BRADY • BEULA TEE FANT • LUELLA E. HOLBERT • JESSIE G. HUDSON • MARY J. BARLOW • DOLORES MERCEDES BROWNE •
Y • ELIZABETH MARSH MCNAIR • MARGARET MAE POWELL • ANNA MARGUERITA TARRYK • GRACE EVELYN BRYANT • EDITH MARGUERETE
L • FRANCES E. CEPHAS • SUSAN VIRGINIA CRABTREE • OLIVE KATHERYN DEDEAUX • ALYCE LILLIAN DIXON • EDITH MARIE ELLISON •
NIE HART • ELVIRE LOUISE JACKSON • EMMA ELIZABETH JOHNSON • LUCILLE VIRGINIA MAE JOHNSON • CECELIA HARE KELLY • ANNIE
MILLER • DONA MARY PRIMUS • DELORIS LOUISE RUDDOCK • BLANCHE LEONA SCOTT • MARGARET PERKINS SIMMONS • CHRISTINA
NE WEBB • DORA MAE WILLIAMS • VERTILE JESSIE MAE WILLIAMS • EDNA JOSEPHINE CROSS BURTON • GLADYS SELUCIA CLAYTON •
GREENLEE • DENA MALISSA HUTCHINS • FLORIDA BELL JACKSON • ELIZABETH OLA LAMB • FANNIE BOYD LITTLE • JOSIE MAE LOWE •
A SMITH • ESSIE MAE WATTS • WILLIE MAE WILLIAMS • ETHEL MAE WINGO • SYLVIA ETHEL ARMSTRONG • WILMA EVONNE BARNES •
LDRED E. CASON • ANNIE OLIVIE CRAWL • LOLA BERNICE DAVIS • MARY F. DAVIS • BERTHA CRAIG DUPREE • CLEOPATRA ELAINE EVANS
TUS CLYDE GREENE • VERNELLE ANNALEE HANNAH • JULIA CATHERINE HARRIS • NELLIE RUTH HARMON • FLORINE J. HILL • SADIE LOU
ERESA O'BRYANT • BEULAH HELEN PATTEN • MARY LOUISE PETERSON • ELOUISE ALGATIA PINKNEY • ARDELLA CODY PITTS • ELOUISE
D TANNER • BESSIE GLADYS TURNER • CLAIRE LILLIA WATERS • LEOLA L. WHEAT • LETTIE ROBERTA WILLIAMS • CLARA EMMA WILSON
U BOWEN • LILA VIRGINIA BURT • GLORIA HERMOLINE CARR • PINKIE COLLIER • ARJEAN CONNER • ANNA MAE COUCH • RUTHANNA
FLY • GWENDOLYN FREEMAN • JACQULYN FULLER • WINONA FULLER • CECILIA DELPHINE GOLDSBY • CALLIE NICHOLS GRANT • ANNIE
HORACE • MATTIE LAURA JACKSON • RUTH SARVER JACOBS • GEORGIA ELLA KITCHEN • JUANITA ROSE LANE • RUTH ELLEN LEWIS •
LETHELMA MOORE • HELEN MAREA NORRIS • THELMA LEE O'KELLY • ELLA LEE PARKER • SARAH ANTOINETTE PARKER • ELIZABETH M.
RGARET GLENN SALES • EDNA RANDOLA SAMPLES • DOROTHY H. SCOTT • GRACE BERNICE SIMPSON • MARY JANE SMITH • GUSSYE
LYN YERGER • BRIDGET VIOLA BIVENS • LUCILLE FRANCES BUTLER • DORIS M. NORREL CABLE • BENNYE BARBARA DANIELS • BLANCHE
LL • HAZEL D. MOORE • CORDELIA LUCILLE TOLLIVER • CLARA MARIE WEBB • MARY L. WHITING • DOLLY B. WOODS • HAZEL EVELYN
RSON • TOMMYE RUTH BERRY • DOLLIE ELIZABETH JACKSON • MINTHA JONES • LAVINIA CLEORA LOWERY • EVELENA O'DELL • GOLDA
A WASHINGTON • CECIL IONE WILSON • HENRIETTA G. ADAMS • JENNETTA SCHOOLER BLYTHE • EMMA H. BROCK • EFFIE CHAMBERS •
S • VIVIAN GENEVA HAYDEN • JULIA M. JACKSON • SARA ELIZABETH LONGMIRE • GRANT ESTHER MARSHALL • EVELYN EVA MILLER •
AE BELL • BESSIE MAE CARTER • MARIE DORA CHARLOT • MARGIE ANTOINETTE CHESTANG • LIDDIE MAE DUNCAN • ALTHEA VERONICA
JONES • CATHERINE GENEVA LANDRY • ANNIE MAE LAWSON • ELFREDA ST. ANNE LEBEAU • MARY MCCLAIN • CHARLOTTE M. MCCULLUM
BETH PICKETT • ANNETTE W. SIMMONS • MENTHIE ROBBIE TALBERT • MALINDA ANN WASHINGTON • SHIRLEY HERTIESINE WEAREY •
RPHY MATTHEWS • ANNIE BEULAH MOORE • FAYRINE R. MURRAY • MARY CATHERINE NAILOR • EMILY OLIVE NOISETTE • THELMA ALICE
HENRYNE TAYLOR • GRACE MARGARET WHYTE • ELEANOR ANN WILSON • VIVIAN WINIFRED YOUNG • LAURA AMELIA BIAS • BEVERLY
ANCE MURIEL HERNANDEZ • ELOISE B. MCNEELEY • MARY ELIZABETH MOODY • ELSIE JEANNETTA OLIVER • ANNIE LEE BRACEFUL • EDNA
S LEE HAIRSTON • BERNICE HESTER • MADELYN LOU HUDGINS • PHILISTA JOHNSON • ADELLA KING • CELESTINE MATHIS • BETTYE JEAN
CE EUNICE HUGGAR • VIRGINIA MARCELLINE LANE • VERNIE MAE SMITH • ELNORA ALTA WALLACE • LEONA ABRAM • LOUISE RITA BRUCE
IFFIN • ADLEASE HARDING • MABEL LUCILLE HASKIN • OLIVIA JOHNSON • MINNIE PEARL LACKEY • MILDRED FREDONIA MONTGOMERY
BERLY • DOROTHY COX • VIOLET W. HILL • ANNA MAE JACKSON • PEARLINE MCKELL • FLORENCE VERLILIAN SCALES • HELEN SHERON
NAH WILLIAMS • ALBERTA ORA BRADLEY • GERALDINE EUNICE HERNDON • MABLE VIRGINIA NEVELS • EVELINA O'DELL • DORIS MOORE
ORIA BUSBY • LILLIAN ADRIANNE BUTTERFIELD • GLADYS EVA DEBMAN • DAISY BELL DINKINS • SYLVIA GILLIS • HESTER GIVENS • ADA
ERMEIL ELMIRA MCMILLAN • DORETHA MILLER • GEORGIANA MORTON • EDITH FRANCES MURRAY • CAROLINE ELIZABETH SMITH •

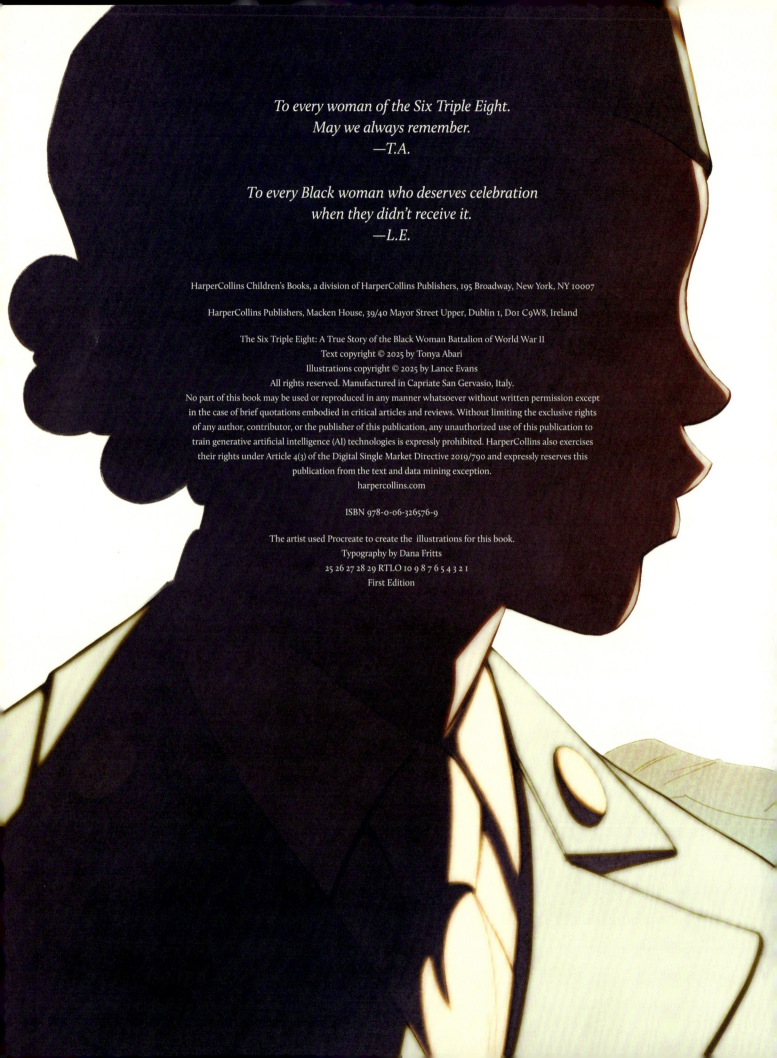

To every woman of the Six Triple Eight.
May we always remember.
—T.A.

To every Black woman who deserves celebration
when they didn't receive it.
—L.E.

HarperCollins Children's Books, a division of HarperCollins Publishers, 195 Broadway, New York, NY 10007

HarperCollins Publishers, Macken House, 39/40 Mayor Street Upper, Dublin 1, D01 C9W8, Ireland

The Six Triple Eight: A True Story of the Black Woman Battalion of World War II
Text copyright © 2025 by Tonya Abari
Illustrations copyright © 2025 by Lance Evans
All rights reserved. Manufactured in Capriate San Gervasio, Italy.
harpercollins.com

ISBN 978-0-06-326576-9

The artist used Procreate to create the illustrations for this book.
Typography by Dana Fritts
25 26 27 28 29 RTLO 10 9 8 7 6 5 4 3 2 1
First Edition

THE
SIX TRIPLE EIGHT

A TRUE STORY OF THE BLACK WOMAN BATTALION OF WORLD WAR II

Written by
TONYA ABARI

Illustrated by
LANCE EVANS

HARPER
An Imprint of HarperCollinsPublishers

Maybelle Rutland Campbell
Charity Adams Earley
Elizabeth Barker Johnson
Lena Derriecott King
Anna Mae Robertson
Deloris Louise Ruddock

Six courageous women enlisted into the United States Women's Army Corps and promised to protect and serve. As did the nearly 860 predominantly Black women of the 6888th Central Postal Directory Battalion.

They had one very special mission during World War II: *save the United States mail*!

In 1942, the United States was deep into battle.

When millions of men left for the war, they also left plenty of vacancies on the home front. From mathematicians to nurses to government employees, jobs needed filling . . . but who would step into these critical roles?

Women, that's who! Ready and able to replace male workers who left for the battlefront, women worked in shipyards, factories, railroads, and many other places! They performed duties on foreign soil as well as at home, making life better for troops and their families.

Inspired by the Rosie the Riveter poster, women were contributing to the war effort. And Black women—Black Rosies—were contributing, too. They did the home front and wartime jobs that may not have seemed important, but really were. There was nothing these women couldn't do!

But many people thought it was impossible for Black women to contribute to the military at all. The army was segregated like much of the country, which still did not allow Blacks and whites to attend the same schools, sit together during concerts, or eat in the same restaurants.

Persistent Black women from all over the country—like Maybelle Rutland Campbell, Charity Adams Earley, Elizabeth Barker Johnson, Lena Derriecott King, Anna Mae Robertson, and Deloris Louise Ruddock—still wanted to enlist.

They knew that there was nothing *they* couldn't do!

Fortunately, ahead of the US entering the war, President Franklin Roosevelt signed Executive Order 8802 in 1941, banning racial discrimination in the defense industry.

Mary McLeod Bethune, an educator and civil rights activist, called upon first lady Eleanor Roosevelt and many other civil rights activists who strongly advocated for Black women getting wartime and military jobs.

Major Black media outlets also helped to find roles for Black women in the newly formed Women's Army Auxiliary Corps.

Military opportunities were now officially knocking—
and Black women answered.

Meanwhile, in Birmingham, England, millions of undelivered pieces of mail and packages were collecting dust in aircraft hangars. Service members noticed that they weren't receiving letters or packages from home. Not getting mail hurt the spirits of the soldiers as well as their families.

Morale was low. Service members were homesick. And families were longing to hear from their loved ones.

The army desperately needed soldiers to manage an overseas postal service that was in complete disarray.

But who was up to this monumental task?

Black women, that's who! 824 enlisted service members and 31 officers were recruited to form the 6888th Central Postal Directory Battalion. The Six Triple Eight was organized into five companies. And the entire directory was led by Major Charity Adams Earley, the first Black woman to achieve the rank of lieutenant colonel in the US Army.

The Six Triple Eight first trained in Fort Oglethorpe, Georgia, and then made their way to Birmingham, England, in February of 1945. When they arrived, the battalion fought discrimination and racism on several fronts.

Still, the Six Triple Eight was on a mission; they would not be stopped!

There was mail everywhere! Bags of letters filled hangars and were piled from the floor to the ceiling. The mail room was cold, damp, and poorly lit. *Could they get through this backlog in only six months?*

The mighty battalion was determined. They wore layers of clothes beneath their uniforms and worked long hours, rotating three eight-hour shifts per day. An average of sixty-five thousand pieces of mail were processed each shift using special locator cards, unit numbers, and serial numbers.

The Six Triple Eight developed a motto to stay motivated: *No mail, low morale.* There was nothing that they couldn't do!

The hardworking women of the 6888th Central Postal Directory Battalion completed the mission of redirecting millions of pieces of mail in just three months!

Letters contained messages of hope and survival. Receiving them made soldiers feel like they weren't forgotten. And service members were able to request items and get care packages from family and friends back home.

No mail, low morale.

The Six Triple Eight was then transferred to Rouen, France. This time to clear a two- to three-year backlog of mail. Using the same energy and strategy from England, they cleared all the mail in just a few months.

After saving the United States' mail during World War II, the Six Triple Eight returned home without any praise or recognition. Although this battalion was the glue for service members and their families, there were no parades, no celebrations, no awards.

But Maybelle, Charity, Elizabeth, Lena, Anna Mae, Deloris, and every hero of the Six Triple Eight knew this:

There was nothing they couldn't do!

Dear Reader,

The Six Triple Eight, or the 6888th Central Postal Directory Battalion, was a unit in the US Women's Army Corps (WAC) that served in World War II. The group of 855 women was led by Major Charity Adams Earley, the highest-ranking Black woman officer in the military, and saved a serious backlog—over 17 million pieces—of US mail! While hard at work, the Six Triple Eight had a slogan, "No mail, low morale," because they knew how important receiving and sending mail was to the soldiers who were thousands of miles away from their loved ones.

If you can see it, you can be it!

Although the topic of war is very complex, I wrote this book because I wanted to honor the brave women of the Six Triple Eight. I also did not want this vital part of history to be overlooked. The lasting impact of these women's contributions has ushered in significant strides for Black women and girls in the military and civilian life.

—Tonya Abari

THE LEGACY OF THE SIX TRIPLE EIGHT

The Black women of the 6888th Central Postal Directory Battalion played a major role in World War II. They were heroes—all while fighting racism and discrimination in the armed forces and at home. When members of the Six Triple Eight arrived stateside in 1946, there were no parades or celebrations.

Speaking to younger women at a ceremony on February 25, 2009, a 6888th veteran said:

"You are standing on our shoulders.
But let me tell you what our pride is: seeing you
young women who have succeeded since us."

—Private First Class Gladys Schuster Carter (February 15, 1922–June 30, 2009),
cofounder of the National Association of Black Military Women

Members of the 6888th Central Postal Directory Battalion were not just soldiers. They were also friends, aunties, mothers, teachers, grandmothers, volunteers, and community members who ranged in age from seventeen to fifty-two. While every contribution from those who were in this battalion is important, here are some interesting facts about the women who were mentioned in this book and publicly honored.

LIEUTENANT COLONEL CHARITY ADAMS EARLEY (1918-2002) Earley became the first Black woman to achieve officer rank. Because the US Army was segregated until 1948, she led the only company of Black and Brown WAC overseas. Commanding the 6888th Central Postal Directory Battalion, Lieutenant Colonel Adams Earley also raised the morale during both overseas missions by creating an optimal social environment, including a beauty salon for the battalion to use when off duty from their mail operation.

CORPORAL ALYCE DIXON (1907-2016) After serving in the war, Dixon worked for the Census Bureau and the Pentagon while also volunteering for Washington Hospital Center and what's known today as Howard University Hospital until retiring in 1972. In 2014, at 107 years old, she was greeted at the Oval Office by then president Barack Obama. At the time, Dixon was the oldest living female US World War II veteran.

PRIVATE FIRST CLASS GLADYS SCHUSTER CARTER (1922-2009) After retiring from the US Army, Carter settled near Hampton Roads, Virginia, where she became a founding member of the National Association of Black Military Women.

PRIVATE FIRST CLASS MAYBELLE RUTLAND CAMPBELL (1921-2021) In 2018, at ninety-six years old, Campbell took a Dream Flight. After flying in planes in the WAC when she was just twenty-two years old, she got into the cockpit of a restored 1940s biplane for one final soar.

TECHNICIAN FIFTH GRADE MARY CRAWFORD RAGLAND (1927-2010) At just seventeen years old, Ragland was encouraged by her mother—after seeing a recruiting advertisement in the newspaper—to join the WAC. Ragland was among other women of the 6888th Battalion honored by Freedom Team Salute. A month later, Mary and other service women were addressed by then first lady Michelle Obama at Arlington National Cemetery in 2009.

PRIVATE FIRST CLASS DELORIS LOUISE RUDDOCK (1923-2021) After the war, Ruddock used the GI Bill to attend fashion school in New York City. After a short career in fashion, Ruddock transitioned to the banking industry before retiring and returning to live in Maryland, her home state, where she had attended the historic Cardozo High School in Washington, DC.

REPORTING FOR DUTY: A TIMELINE

MAY 1941: US Representative Edith Nourse Rogers (Massachusetts) recommends forming the Women's Army Auxiliary Corps.

JANUARY 1943: The Women's Army Corps (WAC) is created from the Women's Army Auxiliary Corps, allowing women to receive the same ranks, pay, privileges, and benefits as the men in the US Army.

1944: With the help of Mary McLeod Bethune and First Lady Eleanor Roosevelt, Black newspapers across the country challenge the US Army to include opportunities for Black women.

FEBRUARY 3, 1945: The 6888th Battalion sets sail, first stopping in Glasgow, Scotland, before arriving in Birmingham, England, on February 11 to a backlog of nearly seventeen million pieces of mail.

MAY 1945: The battalion is transported to Rouen, France, to clear another backlog of mail. There they march through the city and receive great treatment from the locals.

OCTOBER 1945: After clearing the Rouen, France, backlog, they arrive in Paris, France.

FEBRUARY 1946: The Six Triple Eight returns stateside to Fort Dix, New Jersey. There is no public celebration or initial recognition for the battalion.

MARCH 3, 2009: In celebration of Women's History Month, the Six Triple Eight is honored at the Women in Military Service for America Memorial at Arlington National Cemetery by then president Barack Obama and first lady Michelle Obama. Alyce Dixon and Mary Crawford Ragland are in attendance.

MARCH 15, 2016: The Six Triple Eight is inducted into the US Army Women's Foundation Hall of Fame.

NOVEMBER 30, 2018: Sculptor Eddie Dixon unveils the 6888th Battalion monument at Fort Leavenworth, Kansas, where five former soldiers from the battalion are present (Maybelle Rutland Campbell, Elizabeth Barker Johnson, Lena Derriecott King, Anna Mae Robertson, and Deloris Louise Ruddock).

MAY 2019: A plaque to honor the Six Triple Eight is presented in the UK and featured in Birmingham's Black Heritage Walks Network.

MARCH 14, 2022: Then President Joseph Biden signs into law a bipartisan bill to award the 6888th Battalion the US Congressional Gold Medal.

GLOSSARY

The Second World War (World War II) was a global conflict that involved over fifty nations. It began in 1939 when Nazi Germany invaded Poland. After six years, the Allies defeated the Axis powers in 1945. Here is some more information about the terms and people in this book:

battalion: A large body of troops, or groups of soldiers in the armed forces

Black Rosies: A term that represents the more than half a million Black women who worked on the home front during the war effort. The iconic original *Rosie the Riveter* image represents America's hardworking women; however that image did not show the diversity in America's female workforce. Black women worked in shipyards, factories, railroads, government offices, and many more places.

civil rights: A person's birthright of freedom and equality. In the United States, these rights are protected by the US Constitution. The movement for racial equality peaked in the United States during the 1950s and 1960s, which resulted in Congress enacting the Civil Rights Act of 1964, which further protects citizens from unlawful discrimination.

discrimination: The act or practice of treating a person differently based on factors like skin color, race, gender, age, economic status, or ability

Eleanor Roosevelt: The first lady of the United States from 1933 to 1945. She, along with Mary McLeod Bethune, pushed for the Women's Army Auxiliary Corps to enlist Black women.

Executive Order 8802: An executive order issued to end discrimination in the defense program, allowing women and men of any racial or ethnic background to join the US Armed Forces

Franklin D. Roosevelt: The 32nd president of the United States, who issued Executive Order 8802

home front: The activities of civilians at home when the nation is at war

Mary McLeod Bethune: An American educator and civil and women's rights activist who was an adviser to President Franklin D. Roosevelt

morale: The emotional well-being of an individual or group. During war, a soldier's morale can be affected because they are often in a different environment and go weeks, months, and sometimes years without talking to their loved ones. Mail service helps soldiers to communicate with family and friends back home, often boosting their morale.

segregation: A separation or isolation based on factors such as race, class, religion, or ethnicity. Segregation laws in the US once meant that Black people couldn't drink from the same water fountains, attend the same schools, or eat in the same restaurants as white people, and received lower wages.

Women's Army Corps (WAC): A military branch that gave women in the US Army the same ranks, privileges, and benefits as their male counterparts

FURTHER READING

Army Women's Foundation. "6888th Central Postal Directory Battalion 1944–1946." www.awfdn.org/trailblazers/6888th.

Boyd, Deanna, and Kendra Chen. "The History and Experience of African Americans in America's Postal Service." Smithsonian National Postal Museum, May 2022. postalmuseum.si.edu/research-article/the-history-and-experience-of-african-americans-in-america%E2%80%99s-postal-service.

The Buffalo Soldier Educational and Historical Committee. "The 6888th Central Postal Directory Battalion Monument." Women of the 6888th Central Postal Battalion. www.womenofthe6888th.org/the-6888th-monument.

———. "The Women of the 6888th Central Postal Directory Battalion." www.womenofthe6888th.org.

Cooke, Gregory S., dir. *Invisible Warriors: African American Women in World War II* (Charlie Horse Productions, 2022), 1 hr. www.invisiblewarriorsfilm.com.

Hughes, T. A., and John Graham Royde-Smith. "World War II, 1939–1945." *Encyclopedia Britannica*, January 1, 2025. www.britannica.com/event/World-War-II.

Michaels, Debra, ed. "Mary McLeod Bethune," National Women's History Museum, 2015. www.womenshistory.org/education-resources/biographies/mary-mcleod-bethune.

National Association of Black Military Women. www.nabmw.org.

———. "The Rosies." www.nabmw.org/the-rosies.

National Park Service. "6888th Central Postal Directory Battalion," November 2, 2023. www.nps.gov/articles/000/6888th.htm.

Peters, Gerhard, and John T. Woolley. "Remarks by the First Lady at Arlington National Cemetery." The American Presidency Project, March 3, 2009. www.presidency.ucsb.edu/documents/remarksthe-first-lady-arlington-national-cemetery.

Poe, Diandra. "6888th Central Postal Directory Battalion (Women's Army Corps) – BHM." Glass Soldier, February 14, 2014. www.glasssoldier.org/6888th-central-postal-directory-battalion-womens-army-corps-bhm.

Reese, Malchom, dir. *The Six Triple Eight* (Lincoln Penny Films, 2019), 1 hr., 12 min. www.pbs.org/video/the-six-triple-eight-ji6hnl.

Thaxton, Melissa, and Jennifer Dubina. "A Different Kind of Victory: The 6888th Central Postal Battalion." National Museum of the United States Army. www.thenmusa.org/articles/a-different-kind-of-victory-the-6888th-central-postal-directory-battalion.

MARJORIE RANDOLPH SUGGS • CATHERINE E. TURNER • MARION VANORKEY • BREDA VIOLET WILLIAMS • HEATHER RILEY WITHERS
BERNICE A. AUGUSTINE • DOROTHY ELIZABETH BANKS • MARY HORTENSA BANKSTON • DOROTHY AGNES BARTLETT • ADELINA HARRI
THEODORA D. BRYANT • LILLIAN ELNORA CABBELL • MARCELLA LEE CANTY • GLADYS SCHUSTER CARTER • MADELINE A. COLEMAN
GWENDOLYN CLARK DEANE • EMMA SCOTT DEFREESE • HARRIETT ELAINE DOUGLAS • IZETTA M. DOUGLAS • LULAR RACHEL DOWNING
EVELYN LOUISE FRAY • CRESCENCIA GARCIA • MATTIE GARRETT • MARIE BIRDELL GILLISSLEE • BERNICE M. GRANT • MARY ELIZABETH
• RUTH ELMAH JAMES • EVANGELINE GERTRUDE JEFFREY • ADA LOUISE JENNINGS • ALEASE EILEEN JOHNSON • LAURETTA JOHNSON
• DOROTHY ELIZABETH LOUNDS • ETHEL CHRISTINA LOVING • EVELYN BERNICE LOZI • FANNIE E. LYNCH • GERTRUDE MARTIN MARSH
MCWHORTER • AUDREY MEYERS • CHARLA M. MITCHELL • KATHERINE A. MITCHERSON • NORMA KATHERINE MOORE • BEATRICE ROSET
JUNE REEVES • LOUISE ALMENTA REID • MYRTLE A. RHODEN • DORIS S. RICHARDSON • VELMA ANN RIDDICK • BEULAH EUGENIA ROB
SHOWELL • CALLIE KATRINA SMITH • DORIS ELIZABETH STEWART • ROSE STONE • NAOMI STUDDARD • BLANCHE VIRGINIA SWANTNER
• SARA E. WILLIAMS • HELEN W. WOOD • DOROTHY GLORIA YOUNG • SALLIE B. ALEXANDER • ELIZABETH BERNICE BARKER • ODESSA AL
LOUISE GLENN • FRANCES MYRTLE GRAY • ESTHER DELOIS HALL • VERNESE VIRGINA HAYES • CATHERINE ROSANDER HINTON • LUCILE
LEDBETTER • LOTTIE SUE MILLS • FANNIE CLARINE SMITH • INEZ NAOMI STROUD • EFFIE CLARK SUTTON • SARAH GAITHER TAYLOR •
KATHERINE S. BOLDEN • HATTIE BOYCE • CLAUDIA DRUCILLA BRAXTON • VIVIAN MAE BROWN • LOUISE ELLENE BRYERS • ANNA L. BYB
DEWITT • CARROLL MAE EDWARDS • VIVIAN FITZSIMMONS • IRENE H. GARNER • MILDRED REBECCA GATES • DOROTHY MARY GATLIFF
CATHERINE CAROLINE JOHNSON • EUNICE LEE JOHNSON • TOMMIE MAE JOHNSON • RUTH LUCILLE LOTTIER • IRA MAE HARRIS MCCLOU
• HAZEL NORMAN • AZALIA I. WILLIAMS OLIVER • MONIESAH PETWAY • DURAY MAE PRESTWOOD • DOROTHY QUEEN • DOROTHY MAE R
• VIRGINIA ANN SINGLETON • ALBERTA MYKE SMITH • DARNELA BERNICE SMITH • DORIS JOSEPHINE SMITH • RUBYE MARIE SMITH •
WARDEN • ALBERTA DOROTHY WASHINGTON • RUTH LELAN WYATT • BLANCHE ALBRITTON • IZONA J. BROWN • OPAL DORIS BROWN • I
MAGGIE MAE MCCLENTON • IRENE MORROW • ANNA W. MOSS • GUTHRIE H. ROWLAND • ANJENETTIE SMITH • MABEL FRANCIS SNEED • T
ANDERSON • MARY ADLINE ARTIST • LOUISA BALLS • EDNA BASTIN • LENA DERRIECOTT BELL • BLANCHE VIOLA BERKS • CAROLYN MO
CORNWELL • FRANCES VERNON CREWS • CATHERINE JANE CRUMP • VIOLET DABNEY • RHODA ANN DANIEL • ELSIE ALVERNA DANNALS
EVANS • OPHELIA MAE EWINGS • ERMAYNE SANATA FAULK • ALVIA FERGUSON • ALICE OLIVIA FORD • ARENA THERESA GLOVER • HELEN
HARRIS • WILLIE MARIE JACKSON • ISOFINE JACOBS • BEBE C. JOHNSON • HESSIE JOHNSON • ELAINE VIOLA JONES • FRANCES C. JO
HENRIETTA LUCAS • TRYPHENA TERESA MANCE • BERENICE ELISABETH MARSETT • JULIA MCNEAL • MARY PRISCILLA MONROE • ELIZAB
LEE PINKETT • THELMA ELIZABETH PURDY • DOROTHY LOUISE REID • JULIA A. RICH • ALEESE JUANITA ROBINSON • JUANITA GERTRUDE I
• ELEANOR FRANCES SULLIVAN • CLEOLA E. GRAY • MARGOIT MICHELE TOWNSEND • CORNELIA DOLORES WARFIELD • DOROTHY ELIZAE
CATHERINE WRIGHT • MARY PURNELL YOUNG • ANNIE M. REESE • CHARITY EDNA ADAMS • ALVA B. BACOTE • LUCILE M. BALLOON • I
LIPSCOMB • VIVIAN ALICE MAZYCK • CAROLYN BLONDELL POOLE • ANN E. SMALLS • ERMENE ELIZABETH TAYLOR • JENNIE RUTH TUR
SYLVERTLA DAILEY • LIMA JUSTINE HOWARD • ILDA RUTH LEAGUE • CORA DEVERNE MADISON • MARY MARGURITE MARTIN • GEORGIA
• FLORENCE MARIE COLE • MARGUERITE J. ELLIS • JUANITA JEWEL GOODLOE • MARY LOUISE HILL • MILDRED LOIS HOOPER • PAULENE A
• JERRELL LAWRENCE • CATHERINE LEE • LUCILLE LEWIS • RUBY LEE MCCLUNG • MARTHA ANNA MCKNIGHT • OPHELIA MILLS • HELEN BI
• ESSIE LEE PENN • MILDRED ELIZABETH PETERSON • CALONIA V. POWELL • JEWELL G. RETTIG • MINERVA LORAINE REVERNAL • EDDIE
SMITH • ROSE STUART • MILLIE MARY TAYLOR • JOHNNIE MAE WALTON • MYRTLE ELIZABETH WRIGHT • MABLE JEANNETTE ZENON • A
CORNELIA BOWDEN • LILLIE MAE BRATCHER • CATHERINE G. BROWN • MARY ELMIRA BUSTER • IRENE VIRGINIA CARR • ELIZABETH CA
BERTIE MARIE EDWARDS • ISABELLA P. EVANS • ANNIE TURNER FINLEY • PHYLLIS INEZ GALLOWAY • ANNE BYRNEL GARRISON • EDITH PA
MAE JACKSON • FRANCES GERTRUDE JEFFERSON • HAZEL CORDELIA JENNINGS • ROMAY CATHERINE JOHNSON • LEONA VIRGINIA JONI
NANNIE MEDLEY • ELIZABETH CHRISTINA MOORE • JENNIE DEE MOTON • LOUISE TYLER PENNY • ANNIE LUCILLE PLEASANTS • RUTH ELI
MYKE A. MITCHELL SMITH • AUBREY ANNETTE STOKES • VASHTI B. TONKINS • MARCELL BOOKER WILSON • ARLETHEA MOLLIE CAWTHORN
BELLE MARTIN • PHOEBE ELAINE MILLER • LUCILLE A. POINDEXTER • LERAH N. SAUNDERS • CLARA BELLE SIMON • SALLIE M. SMITH